Painting Brooklyn Stories

paintings **Nina Talbot**

poems **Esther Cohen**

Pleasure Boat Studio: A Literary Press
New York

PAINTING BROOKLYN STORIES of Immigration and Survival

Nina Talbot © 2010

Paintings **NINA TALBOT**

Poems **ESTHER·COHEN**

An exhibition of paintings, drawings, photographs, objects, books
and audio recordings of oral histories from 1999-2010 organized
for the Brooklyn Historical Society as part of the Public Perspective series of
community-curated exhibits.

Public Perspectives is made possible through the generous support of the
Lily Auchincloss Foundation and FHL Bank, with additional support from Kress Foundation and HBO.

September 16, 2010-February 26, 2011
The Brooklyn Historical Society
128 Pierrepont Street
Brooklyn, NY 11201-2711
(718) 222-4111
www.brooklynhistory.org

Artist Acknowledgements
Brooklyn Historical Society
     Deborah Schwartz
     Kate Fermoile
     Janice Monger
     Sady Sullivan
Rachel Bernstein, Historian, NYU
Esther Cohen, Writer
Laura Tolkow, Flush Left, Graphic Design
Michael Hnatov, Photography
Weeksville Heritage Center, Jennifer Scott & Kaitlyn Greenidge
City Lore, Steve Zeitlin
WNYC, Radio Rookies program

Painting Brooklyn Stories is published by Pleasure Boat Studio: A Literary Press
www.pleasureboatstudio.com

Painting Brooklyn Stories of Immigration & Survival
Nina Talbot/Artist Statement

There are people that one may see only for a few fleeting moments a day, or once a month, or when the blood drive comes to town. We glance quickly at the grocer before tossing him a few coins for the morning paper, or share a smile with our usual barber. Their visages hint at their past and their present—a battle scar, a hijab, platinum blonde hair. Beyond hints of their lives, the tales of their journeys are obscured by their familiar wrinkles and warm greetings. These paintings provide a map to what is beyond everyday faces, and help tell the stories of what these faces have seen.

As one of my subjects, DeNorval, said when I interviewed him: "And I'm still here." Survival can be taken for granted. These portraits depict people I met, survivors all, with compelling scenes from their lives. The characters and scenes overlap in transparent layers, with punchy colors, storefronts, and maps lending a graphic quality to the work.

In these paintings are the faces I have gotten to know, and the stories I have learned about where the people I painted have been and about the things they have lived through. I have tried to paint through the subjects' eyes, tried to see what they have seen.

My path in getting to know them to portray them in my art work is deeply emotional for me, just as the paths of my subjects from where they started to where they have arrived today have been emotional to them. My journey is to learn, to understand and to paint these stories.

While they are capsules of history, these portraits are also praises of the present, and the joy of surviving, thriving, and existing. The paintings tell histories, and they also capture mementos from the present. These present conditions are borne from history, and they have contributed to identities that reflect, embrace, or attempt to forget the pained past.

My work is an attempt to capture what they saw and heard and felt in the rich and complex lives they lived—all around the world, and, finally, here in Brooklyn.

Introduction
Rachel Bernstein

What does it mean to be a city of immigrants? How do we make sense of the whole, when the parts are so intensely personal, local, and specific?

One place to start is by looking at the ways individual immigrant stories can echo through time and space—through art—through memory—through neighborhoods—through communities.

Nina Talbot's history-filled portraits begin with intense listening. She listened to her neighbors and friends, including an orphan from Allentown who became known as the historian of Fort Greene; an Iranian Jew with a jewelry shop in Newkirk Plaza; a Tuskegee airman originally from the Caribbean whose mother worked as a servant for a family on Rugby Road near where his son now owns a house; a phlebotomist from Dhaka, Bangladesh, who lives in Midwood; a Park Slope storyteller from Puerto Rico; a writer from Haiti with violent memories of the tonton macoute, now living peacefully in East Flatbush; a musician from Park slope whose 96-year-old mother remembers arriving in New York from Hangzhou, in 1938; a Pakistani Muslim woman living in West Midwood; an artist from Washington D.C. now in Red Hook; and a woman who survived the Mauthausen concentration camp now living in Borough Park.

Their stories are filled with hope and with violence, with powerful cultural traditions and with experiences of discrimination, and they resonate in the daily lives of these Brooklynites in 21st-century New York.

This exhibition presents a selection of these immigrant stories in different media and from different angles. Center stage are Talbot's paintings, with elements of each subject's past embedded within. Esther Cohen's poems capture key elements of the stories Talbot collected for her paintings. Many of the storytellers were also interviewed at length by New York University students whose recorded oral histories are excerpted both at audio stations and in print. Photographs, objects, and articles important in individual lives add another layer, while student interpretations of a couple of the stories contribute yet another.

Can a painting be an oral history? I asked Talbot this when we met, for she had, without any introduction to oral history interviewing, been eliciting memories and stories from her subjects and then painting key elements of those stories in her portraits. Oral history is at heart a special kind of listening—listening with an intensity of focus and a commitment of time rarely found today. How closely do these portraits reflect the "voice" and the memories of the subjects?

The juxtaposition of art and saved object, of stories told and retold in first-person recordings, in paint and on paper, affords multiple opportunities to reflect upon these questions. The exhibit's layers allow viewers to make connections among the stories, and lend a valuable perspective on what it means to live in a city of immigrants.

Introduction
Kate Fermoile & Janice Monger / Brooklyn Historical Society

Nina Talbot paints lively portraits of her neighbors and the people she encounters in Brooklyn who have life stories that extend far beyond their resident borough. Talbot's paintings communicate the diversity of Brooklyn through focusing on individual stories of immigrants, demonstrating how each person represents worlds of experiences that they carry with them into their lives in Brooklyn.

Painting is a process of storytelling and community building for this artist. She gets to know her subjects through interviews, hearing about their stories in Brooklyn and what led them here. Words inform the paintings, and impressions from these individuals' life stories become part of the imagery. Nina Talbot's paintings swirl with colors and memories. These energetic works provide glimpses into the lives of Brooklynites who have arrived from places all around the world and from vastly different situations. The artist offers her interpretation of what her subjects have shared with her, and she expresses their stories of strength.

The Brooklyn Historical Society is interested in the ways in which individuals contribute to history and the many different ways in which history can be interpreted and represented. For this exhibit and publication, Nina Talbot worked with oral historian Rachel Bernstein to incorporate the carefully recorded stories of these individuals in their own voices. Talbot also collaborated with poet Esther Cohen, who offers another form of interpretation with her words, distilling impressions of the great depth of these individuals and their stories. This exhibit honors individuals' struggles and strengths and explores the differing ways stories of survival may be recorded, interpreted and celebrated.

Nina Talbot and her collaborators have approached this project with tremendous creativity, talent, sensitivity and passion. We are pleased to exhibit Painting Brooklyn Stories of Immigration and Survival as the latest installment of the Public Perspectives series at BHS. Central to our mission of connecting the past to the present, Public Perspectives presents community-curated exhibits and programs that give the public an active voice at BHS. Nina Talbot's exhibit captures the collaborative spirit of this program and provides viewers the opportunity to explore powerful representations of the lives of Brooklyn immigrants.

Nina Talbot
Bronx to Brooklyn

She tells stories.
What she sees.
Hearts of her tellers
and their colors, deep
memory colors, vibrant passages
of what life looks like
Persia Guyana Pakistan
And then, always then, Brooklyn.
Harrowing difficult
holocausts, persecutions,
homelessness.
Brooklyn is another beginning.
Nina Talbot
paints stories
of people she meets, interprets
life with her lines and shapes.
Unforgettable blues, then greens.
Her Brooklyn, theirs too.
Deep color of life.
All about
Real Stories

– Esther Cohen

Just Neighborhood Folks

"I lost my husband
and 3 of my children,
but as long
as God allows
I will take just one day
At a time."
Left on a doorstep
I don't know who brought me there
maybe my mother.
I was placed in an orphanage
in Trenton. An elderly
woman Mrs. Spencer
she lived with other blacks.
They were teachers funeral parlor directors
hairdressers.
Mayor Dinkins' father
owned a barbershop

four doors from where i lived.
I went to Trenton Central School. At 18
I married a navy man named
Timothy Loftin. We moved to
Brooklyn and applied to live
In the projects. I moved to
79 North Oxford Walk.
Six children. Three died.
My husband died too.
I worked in the school P.S. 67.
I'm the one
who knows all the history
of this community.
Tragedy happened.
But for me,
it's a day at a time.

Mrs. Loftin

oil/canvas, 36" x 36", 2008

Neighborhood Historian

An ordinary person becomes known and loved by a community
Trenton, NJ, to Fort Greene, Brooklyn

1943 US Air Corps
not accepting black men.
But Fitzroy wanted to fly
anyway. He persisted until
Tuskegee Airmen, black division
of US flyers, took him
in Alabama. Last year, 2009,
he was honored with
other Tuskegee Airmen
at Obama's inauguration.

Fitzroy

oil/canvas, 36" x 36", 2008

Tuskegee Airman
"When you say our country, are you including me?"

Mohammed's father and brother
helped soldiers in the freedom war
between Pakistan and Bangladesh.
It was 1971. His father and brother
were shopping in the village market
when soldiers confronted them.
"We'll have to kill you," they said.
"So kill me," Mohammed's brother said.
Not long after, his father's heart broke,
and he died. His mother cried for years,
and now she's blind. Mohammed Rashid
came to Midwood, in Brooklyn,
in 1990. He lives there now,
with his American family.

Rashid oil/canvas, 36" x 36", 2009

"We have to kill you"

Survivor of Indo-Paki war,
Bangladesh to Midwood, Brooklyn

Ben speaks through
a plexiglass wall
when he fixes watches.
He came to New York
in 1992, Persian Jew,
one of the over 100,000
who left. Less than
8,000 Jews in Iran now.
The government thinks
the Jews are Israeli spies.
Ben ran away to the Pakistani
border. He was caught by police,
sent to jail, tortured. His parents–
it was a miracle–found him
in jail, sent him to Vienna. Then he
made it to New York. Robbed the first
day in the elevator on his way to his
room. He had ten dollars. And
then it was gone. A rabbi bought him
clothes at the Gap. He's married now.
Two sons. He lives
near Kings Highway.

Ben

oil/canvas, 36" x 36", 2009

"You don't know what I went through to get here."

A story of religious persecution and torture
Iran to Midwood, Brooklyn

A lot of good,
a lot of bad.
Desert storm
all black Unit 369, Harlem Hell Fighters.
He walked into
a mine field,
couldn't find
his way back home.
Night sky boom,
scud missiles. Some soldiers
went home in body bags.
Later, when he was
In New Jersey, he was
walking to his car.
A truck hit him
and he died six times.
Lost his legs in New Jersey.
But he's entirely alive, today.

DeNarval Parks oil/canvas, 36" x 36", 2009

"And I'm Still Here."

Fort Greene, Bklyn.

Pakistani homeless man.
Four children
back in Pakistan.
One boy three girls.
Details of a life–
He stayed in stores
in Midwood, another Pakistan.
Many were helped by him.
He gave them homes
when he had one.
And now look–
He's at their mercy.
They offered
to buy him a ticket
back home.
But now he
says he
doesn't have
a home anymore.

Bashir

oil/canvas, 36″ x 36″, 2009

Homeless Sponsor
"Why should they be singing lullabies for me?"

Kashmir to Midwood, Bklyn.

Tanasia lived eight
years, that's all. Just
eight years. For her mother
Tuwana she will always
be alive, always be a child
whose favorite colors
were red pink white.
Always liked to eat
ice cream pizza baked macaroni.
Tanasia Mitchell had
Wilm's tumor, a cancer
in her kidney. For her mother
she will always be
a beautiful young girl.

Tanasia

oil/canvas, 36" x 36", 2010

"If I could have seen her one more time."

Fort Greene, Brooklyn.
Tanasia Mitchell, October 14, 1997-April 5, 2006

Vendors of Newkirk

Newkirk Plaza

Words to describe
this Flatbush place, kind
of old-fashioned shopping mall
when mall meant stores
owned by people, often families,
stores that did not have
familiar names.
(They weren't Starbucks
They weren't McDonalds.)
Stores run by people who came
from one country or another, let's say
Pakistan China India Ukraine,
families
that had the same business.
A relative who knew the business
in the country they came from.
Stores with names that evoke
mystery and real lives, imperfectly lived:
New Royal House of Fabrics
(on Foster Avenue),
Double Dragon
Chinese Restaurant,
Kings and Queens
Hair Studio, Chou Chou
Service, Almac Hardware,
Jamaican Jerk Chicken.
The streets have businesses side by side,

Medical supplies and beauty salons
and everything more or less
that we all need: shoes and sandals
and orthopedics, beautiful silks in bright
orange and pink, dumplings and noodles
and the possibility for transformative
hair, door hinges, fish for dinner.
Someone walking down the street
said that this subway station mall
was built around 1900, the first—
Yes she said it was the first,
maybe it was second or third
but it was there in the beginning—
Open air retail mall in the
Entire country. Right in Flatbush on
Newkirk. The Transit Authority
owns and maintains the deck
and the station. The Department
of Transportation owns
the bridge, and the buildings on the
plaza are owned by shop owners.
The Newkirk stop is an express stop.
Downtown Brooklyn fifteen minutes.
For some of us, shops like the ones
we find on Newkirk are why
we love it here.

If you were able,
if you could
hear stories
of Brooklyn and then
you could paint them,
paint and paint those
traveling stories—
departures arrivals
messy stories of families
and loneliness of what it means
to move one place
to another,
to move to Brooklyn,
to make Brooklyn into home—
and know that your life,
whatever it is,
would become
beautiful, as beautiful
as a painted story.

Beautiful Rita, always
doing hair. So did her Ukrainian mother.
The only girl, Rita was
happy as a child when she was wearing
her plaid coat. A born fashion plate,
she married a jack of many trades: Russian
watchmaker, bakery worker, and, finally,
in a store that cut and sold cushions.
Not too long ago, he died. Their
sons now make designer cushions
in their own store in Chelsea. Rita own Plaza
Hair, a beauty shop on Newkirk Plaza.
She herself
Is unforgettable.

Rita Of Plaza Hair

oil/canvas, 60" x 54", 2005

"I was so happy, once."

From Lvov, Ukraine to Brighton Beach, Brooklyn

Susan of Double-Dragon Chinese Restaurant

oil/canvas, 55" x 54", 2006

From China to Midwood.

Nick of Newkirk Liquors

oil/canvas, 44" x 44", 2006

From Bensonhurst to Midwood.

Leon's Fantasy Cuts

oil/canvas, 50" x 50", 2005

From Ukraine to Midwood.

Fatima of Royal House Fabrics

oil/canvas, 42" x 34" 2006

From Pakistan to Midwood.

Sasha of Alex's Shoes

oil/canvas, 36" x 36" 2006

From Ukraine to Brighton Beach, Brooklyn

Paul of Almac Hardware oil/canvas, 48"x54", 2006

Flatbush, Brooklyn

Generations of Brooklyn

Born in Washington, DC,
over seventy years ago.
The city was the beginning
long integration process.
Verna saw her mother,
a domestic worker,
push a white woman on the bus.
The woman wanted Verna's mother
to sit in back where she belonged.
And she said no. Verna has been
a painter all her life. Forty years
in Red Hook projects, earning
her living, raising four children,
painting painting.

Verna

oil/canvas, 48" x 44" 2002

"The gates over the projects are beautiful."

From Washington, DC, to Red Hook, Brooklyn

David Rand–
my father-in-law–
father of my husband Mark.
David almost didn't survive
Auschwitz. Right before
the American soldiers
came to free the prisoners,
SS officers
ran their Jewish prisoners
through the woods
wanting to kill
more of them
before the Allies arrived.
David watched his brother die,
shot by the SS.
He didn't want to leave him there,
so he fell on the ground
pretending to be dead.
He hid in the woods for several
days. Later he met Eva
in a camp for displaced persons.
They married
and moved to Brooklyn, where
they had 5 children. David ran a shoe store
In Williamsburg.

Many years later, Mark ran a marathon
in honor of his father's run for his life
through the German woods.
When he got home, he cried.

A1837/David   oil/canvas, 48" x 44", 2003

"My life was destroyed."

From Mukachevo, Czechoslovakia, to Williamsburg, Brooklyn.

Serena in Mauthausen Camp after Hungary.
Finally liberated 1945 by Black American soldiers.
Her heroes for life. Hungary, Germany,
Borough Park, Brooklyn.
Prejudice surprised her.
Single mother 8 children, Serena
arrived in Brooklyn. It was 1946.
Kosher cook for hotels. She spoke
Yiddish and Hungarian. No English.
Most Sundays, her relatives
came to see her
at Amnon's Kosher Pizza.
107 when she died.

Serena

oil/canvas, 48"x48", 2003

"I could kiss their feet."

From Balmazuvaros, Hungary, to Borough Park, Brooklyn

Tih Lou, Fran's mother
(Fran is a Park Slope musician,
two children) born
Hangzhou, China.
She was young when the Japanese
invaded, in the thirties. Her family
ran to the mountains. A miracle
they survived. She
came to New York in 1938,
making Chinese lampshades
and dresses for her husband's
cousin's business. Later,
she and her husband owned
Jimmy's Grocery, in Harlem.
Tih Lou, now ninety-nine,
lives near there today.

oil/canvas, 44" x 36", 2002

"Mom was one of the first Chinese woman immigrants to become a US citizen in New York."

Fran Onne (daughter), Park Slope, & Tih Lou, From Hangzhou, China, to Park Slope, Brooklyn

Placida Molet,
daughter of slaves
in Puerto Rico,
adopted Daniel at the age of four
right after his birth mother died.

Placida Molet became his mother.
"She was my everything," he said.
She died in 1967, after Daniel
married. Daniel had four children of his own.
Placida sang slave songs
to soldiers in Puerto Rico as they went
to war. She sang in the hospital,
danced there, too, until she died.
His life, his memories of Placida,
his family, and his work
for the Taino people
of Puerto Rico,
his first home.

pastel, 30 x 22", 2002

"She was my everything."

From Vieques, Puerto Rico (mother), to Gowanus, Brooklyn

Taino Nation of the Antilles
America has denied Taino Culture
and the recognition of the
Native American
saying it is
extinct. Not only
are we alive,
but our DNA is
still dominant
Native American
girl.

Daniel's parents wedding picture

"She was my
everything."
Placida Matos, daughter of slaves
in Puerto Rico, who befriend y
Daniel's mother who adopted Daniel
when he was four years old after
his mother died. She was ld after
Sange   that had sang slaves
               Sange in Puerto Rico. Hey
               She was   not he was
               Daniel died it natural.
               Placida died it natural.
               was already an independent
               children. By the next day
               Placida was dancing and
               the Martial arts raising and
                         stuff.

"Just people
are all around you,"
they told Daniel,
"who brighten
the way   embrace,
free from which the
wood is such with
their light, he like
to help people else
them out of darkness
to help themselves."

She is a religious
Muslim woman,
Koran teacher.
Many doctors
in Anna's family.
She has plans: Once she
finds her way through
this society – she's
already been in Brooklyn
for ten years – for her
daughters to be
American doctors.

Asma

pastel, 22"x30", 2003

From Islamabad, Pakistan, to Midwood, Brooklyn

Her grandmother was afraid
she'd be shot. So Lahiny didn't
go to Haitian school, didn't
want to dodge the bullets
of the Tonton Macoute.
The words mean Uncle Gunnysack
but in Haiti everyone knows
the Tonton Macoute is evil,
shooting killing years and years.
Lahiny came to Brooklyn.
A writer now, she tells
her own stories.

Lahiny

acrylic/canvas, 24" x 20", 2004

"You don't know who's listening."

From Jacmel, Haiti, to East Flatbush, Brooklyn.

One night after the earthquake in Kobe, I traveled by taxi,
then three hours on foot, to find my parents' house.
Thankfully, they survived.

My Fragile Art it is a series of photographs:
plaster Statues of Liberty, kicked and
stepped on, representing myself.
In this big and international city, a part of me
has changed because of all the people and
all the cultures. My transformation is
like what happened to the plaster statues I made.

acrylic/canvas, 42" x 48" , 2004

**"I traveled one night by taxi, and then three hours on foot, to
reach my parent's house after the earthquake in Kobe, Japan, in 1995.
Thankfully, they were alive."**

From Kobe, Japan, to Bedford-Stuyvesant, Brooklyn.

Even in Guyana
where they're side by side,
the races all fight. She was ten years old.
Koreen said the east indians
wanted to beat the black
out of her. Thirty years later,
the Africans wanted to
beat the indian out of her daughter.

Guyana,
where she was born,
where she was from.
Word meaning land
of many waters.

6 peoples–
African East Indian
Amerindian Chinese
Portuguese European.
Her mother Edna Wong,
Amerindian and Chinese.
African and Portuguese
Father. She is married to
Samuel. Big mix too.
4 children. 6
grandchildren. Koreen
has a Dutch goddess sister
named Fabiola. Koreen
Jones has a big identity.

pastel, 22″ x 30″, 2005

"The name Guyana is an Amerindian word meaning 'Land of many waters'"

From Demerara, Guyana, to Fort Greene, Brooklyn, 2004.